AF471769

THE BEADS OF LOVE

A ROSARY

A meditation on the life of Jesus and a devotion to the Blessed Virgin Mary, his Mother

DAVID GENTLE

GRACEWING

First published in 2006 by Connor Court Publishing Pty Ltd, Australia

This edition published in the United Kingdom and Europe in 2007 by:

Gracewing Publishing
2 Southern Avenue
Leominster
Herefordshire HR6 0QF
www.gracewing.co.uk

ISBN: 978 0 85244 156 5

Printed in England

CONTENTS

FOREWORDS

Cardinal George Pell

The Rosary is an ancient Catholic prayer which is still suitable for Australian Christians today. More recently, too, an increased number of Christians have come to appreciate the importance of meditation, or personal prayer, perhaps influenced by Eastern styles of meditation.

Christians have their own rich tradition of public and private devotions, of meditation and indeed of mysticism. Christians need to know and use these devotions. Often particular ages and cultures develop and adapt the traditional practices to help their prayer.

Father David Gentle's *Beads of Love – A Rosary* is a beautiful approach to a traditional prayer, changed and developed to help today's Christians to pray.

The book recognizes our limited concentration spans and the more important factor that the thirst for God is a constant of human nature. "Our hearts are restless until they rest in you, O God" (St. Augustine).

Devotion to Mary, Mother of God, has a long history in English speaking Christianity, and a longer history in other branches of Western and Eastern Christianity. Mary should be an impetus to ecumenical co-operation, and praying this rosary will not only bring God's blessing upon us, but help bring us all closer together.

+George Cardinal Pell,
Archbishop of Sydney

David Chislett SSC

Christians of all backgrounds will be grateful to Father Gentle for directing us back to the Rosary, a traditional way of praying that takes us to the heart of the Gospel.

The renewal movements of the last forty years restored to the people of God a strong sense of the moving of the Holy Spirit within the individual and within the praying community. In some circles, however, an overemphasis of the "spontaneous" resulted in the loss of simple devotions such as the Rosary, hallowed by centuries of use, that serve as a kind of scaffold for the life of prayer, a scaffold that is mostly helpful in times of trial and spiritual dryness.

Apart from this, the Rosary is packed full of Scripture. Praying it regularly keeps us focussed on the redeeming work of Jesus so that we never forget the price of our salvation, or the glory we are called to share. It is in this way that the extended Scripture reflections written by Father Gentle will nourish many a hungry soul.

The Blessed Virgin Mary is the Mother of all her Son's people, and she prayerfully watches over us as we journey home. In the Rosary our fellowship with her is deepened. Many Christians of diverse traditions are rediscovering the Rosary in our time. This must gladden the heart of her whom Saint Augustine called "the Mother of Unity."

The first explicitly Anglican recommendation of the Rosary was in a book written by Anthony Stafford, a layman, in 1635. The Bishop of London approved the book, and the Archbishop of Canterbury defended it. I am in good company, then, in commending Father Gentle's book to the widest possible readership.

+ David Chislett SSC
Assistant Bishop,
Anglican Catholic Church in Australia

PREFACE

A Glimpse of My Spiritual Journey

My devotion to the Blessed Virgin Mary goes back to my teenage years. My mother had the difficult task of raising three children, with the help of my grandmother. My mother never remarried after the failure of her marriage with my father, whom I never met until I was seventeen years old. It was a hard and lonely life for my mother, who, while loving her mother and children dearly, felt, I'm sure, very unfulfilled, with a deep emptiness in her life. My mother eventully began to search for meaning in her life and began a spiritual journey that led her to the Catholic Faith. At this time in my life, the only religious education that I had was through the religious education program offered in state schools.

One day, my mother came home with a string of Rosary beads. I had never seen a Rosary before, and when she had learnt how to pray the Rosary she then taught me. I felt drawn to the Rosary and began to pray it often. Up to this point, I really hadn't prayed, and, as I prayed the Rosary, my life began to change in a very positive way. I began to feel that Jesus and Mary were with me and guiding me. At this time in my young life, I began my own spiritual search involving the Anglican and Catholic Faiths, and in time I felt that God, through Jesus and Mary, was calling me into service within his church. I developed a deep love for both the Anglican and Catholic expressions of Christianity. In time, I was baptised and later confirmed in the Anglican Church, and this allowed me to express my faith and practice in the wonderful Anglo-Catholic tradition.

As I continued to pray the Rosary, I felt that God was calling me to serve him as a priest. I responded to that call, and, in time, entered St Francis' College, Brisbane, to train for the sacred priesthood. At that time, St Francis' College was steeped in the Anglo-Catholic tradition, and so my love for this expression of the faith and my love for the Rosary continued to grow. The chapel Angelus became a daily call to prayer which drew me closer to Jesus, Mary and the Rosary.

On graduating from St Francis', I returned to the Diocese of Rockhampton, and, after my ordination to the Diaconate, I was sent to the parish of the Callide Valley, Biloela, Central Queensland. The parish priest was a saintly man and a true Anglo-Catholic and I learned a great deal from him that set me in a priestly mould for my future ministry. Morning and Evening Prayer, the daily Mass, the Angelus, and the praying of the Rosary all formed a part of my daily devotions. When the rector became the bishop of Riverina in New South Wales, I continued in the parish as priest-in-charge, until I was transferred to the parish of Gladstone and given pastoral oversight of the former South Gladstone/Miriam Vale parish. Because of my love of teaching Religious Education in schools, I was led by God to become a teacher in the Catholic school system in the Diocese of Rockhampton. I taught in this system for seventeen years and, apart from teaching the usual academic curriculum, I was privileged to teach both formal and informal lessons in Religious Education. During my years with Catholic education, apart from my involvement with faithful Catholic laity, I met several clergy and religious who also had a great love of the Rosary. I deeply cherish the spiritual formation that I received from the Catholic clergy, the Sisters of Mercy, the Sisters of St Joseph and the Franciscan Sisters. Working within the Catholic school system and worshipping with both Catholics and Anglicans gave me a deeper insight into and love of Anglo-Catholicism. Praying in the Anglican Church, I often lit a candle at the Shrine of Our Lady of Walsingham, and still do today at the parish church which also bears the name of our Blessed Lady.

I have been parish priest in the Anglican Dioceses of Rockhampton, Wangaratta and The Murray, in chaplaincies to the Army, Victoria and South Australia Police, to CIAE (Central Queensland University), to colleges and to the Capricornia Chapter of the Order of St Luke the Physician. My ministry of teaching, preaching, counselling, healing and general pastoral care of people have all deepened my sense of vocation and given me a greater understanding of people in their daily lives as they travel through their earthly pilgrimages living and growing in preparation to live fully in their spiritual bodies after death.

In my personal journey through life, I have always prayed regularly and been constantly aware of the presence of God in my life. I have always encouraged people to pray in order to develop their spiritual awareness and relationship with God. As Christians, we believe in things that are seen and unseen and that when we think of Jesus, Mary or any of the saints in reflective or spoken prayer, we call them to be with us. In my work as a clinical psychologist, I often speak to clients about their spirituality in order to impart to them the fact that they are not alone in life, since the force, energy or power of the universe that we call God has sent them to earth on a mission, so their lives are not a mistake but are part of a divine plan. Each person has an overarching purpose in life to be a caring, loving person with a special mission that will be revealed through prayer and meditation, and if one seeks to know it, one will find. Jesus said, "What you sow, you reap", and, because human life is only a chapter of our total lives which are both physical and spiritual, the promise of Jesus will be fulfilled, if not in this life, then in the next.

When counselling clients, I have often encouraged them to say the Rosary, a prayer which gives a structure for people who no longer pray or who are new to prayer. I encourage people to practice the presence of God in their lives – to develop a relationship with Jesus and Mary through contemplative prayer – to "be still and know that I am God.", as the psalmist says.

In my practice of saying the Rosary, and in encouraging others to do the same, I am aware that creative visualization is brought into play as people meditate on the topic of each bead and enter the alpha brainwave and become calm, relaxed and focused. Not only will this practice benefit our physical bodies, such as our cardio-vascular pulmonary systems, but it will benefit our spiritual lives: we communicate with our source of life as we speak with the Father, the Son and the Holy Spirit, and with Mary, Joseph and many other saints.

Religious practice and spirituality have become very popular topics in psychological counselling today. From time to time I get requests from psychology students who are researching for their master's or doctoral thesis, asking me to comment on the importance of religion and spirituality in counselling. I believe that, ultimately, people will only embrace the search for religious and spiritual fulfillment when they discover that life can be very hard and that our time on earth is running out. People will not generally turn to Christ until they are ready to do so. It saddens me that so many people have a "God in the box" approach to life. In times of great need, they pull God out of the box and say to him, "God, you've got to help me", and, when the crisis is over, put him back in the box which is labelled, "To be opened only in an emergency". Sadly, many people tend to be just God-users and not God-faithful. Many Australians, and I'm sure other nationalities as well, are trying desperately to find the meaning of life and have had no joy in their search, just as Monty Python had none in his search for "The Meaning of Life." Could it be that people are simply looking in the wrong places for life's true meaning? If people's spirituality has no greater dimension than the pursuit of wealth and pleasure, then their lives, especially in old age, will have no real spiritual substance to them and these people will not be ready to experience the fullness of God when they exit their physical bodies. Spiritual lives take time to develop and enlightenment eventually comes to those who pursue the light of Christ and bear in mind that all of us who are "in Christ", will also experience our crosses in life.

God is in the business of healing, in turning people's lives around and making things right for them. Through the ministry of Jesus, Mary, other saints, angels and certain spiritually gifted people, God sends healing to those troubled in body, mind and spirit. God either gives people the healing that they desire, or strength to bear their health problems as an earthly cross that they have to carry. I don't pretend to understand the mind of God as to why some people are healed and some are not. It is not my purpose in this brief reflection to fully reveal my life in the Spirit or to delve too deeply into the mysteries of healing, as these are the concerns of a book that is presently being written.

My work in spiritual healing led me into the Order of St Luke the Physician, a multi-denominational, international order of spiritual healers who make the healing that Christ brings a reality in people's lives. For me, personally, my relationship with the Blessed Trinity, with Mary, the angels, and God's other holy ones is nourished and sustained through the sacraments, especially through frequent reception of the Blessed Sacrament, through regularly praying the Rosary and through the practice of the presence of God in my daily life.

In my work as a healer, I combine my practice of psychology with spiritual healing as I believe that the human psyche is a combination of both mind and spirit which both impact on the physical body. I truly believe that I have been called to the healing ministry and this vocation has led me also to St Luke's Healing Foundation, an Australian charity whose mission it is to heal the broken lives of those in need.

I believe that we are not an accident of birth but we are each known by God as one of his children and sent with a specific mission to do some special work of love to help others. The prayer, "Here am I. Send me", should be a request to God to empower us to get on with our special missions. A wise old priest once told me to, "Do great things for Christ and expect great things from Christ." We have to pray asking God to guide us in the work he wants us to do in his name. Christ promised us that if we seek, we will find. We have to remember that, if we do anything to anyone, a positive or a negative thing, it is as if we do it to Christ. As spiritually aware people, we must accept that what we sow, we reap.

Through prayer and meditation, I have come to believe that my special mission is to help homeless young people holistically, to help those who have been beaten up by life, and, through positive interventions, to give them the opportunity to live meaningful lives. Therefore, any monies that are received by me through the sale of this little book will be passed on to St Luke's Healing Foundation for their project Youth Outreach Australia. Of course, if anyone wishes to support the mission of the Foundation to help homeless Australian people, details are available at the last page of this book. Please make the mission of the Foundation a special intention in your prayers, and through this special way you will be an ambassador for Christ to all those needy people. By helping them, you are helping Christ.

For many Christians the praying of the Rosary will be a new experience. The Church has always honoured its saints and those in the Catholic tradition ask for their prayers. All prayer is, of course, directed to God and we always pray "Through Jesus Christ our Lord".

All prayer binds together in love, the church on Earth and the church in Heaven, and, when we ask the saints to pray for us, their prayers join with ours to form a stream of life, a river of prayer that, through Christ, flows to the Father.

God's saints are his holy ones on Earth and in Heaven. The saints in Heaven, and the angels also, continue their ministry of prayer and service in the presence of the Almighty. It is most natural, and common practice, to ask friends to pray for you or for someone else, and when we ask the friends of Jesus who are perfectly alive in Heaven to pray for us, they will not refuse. The church's belief in the communion of saints is a living reality.

Mary, of course, is not just a friend of Jesus: she is his Blessed Mother. In asking her prayers, we honour her as the Mother of the Incarnate God, Jesus. Because God chose Mary to be the Mother of his Beloved Son and because of her great love and devotion to her Child, she has a special place in the hearts of many Christians. Those who ask her prayers are devoted to her as a special saint who fulfilled, and is still fulfilling, a special part in God's plan for the world.

I believe we have entered an age of a new spiritual awakening and many people are searching for ways to deepen their spiritual growth. For those who are truly seeking to develop their spirituality, the Rosary will become an indispensable part.

The Rosary has, I believe, a sacramental nature. The outward visible sign is the Rosary itself, and those who pray the Rosary receive the inward spiritual grace which comes from the prayers and meditation.

God works through both the spiritual and the material to achieve his Divine purposes. He works through the flesh and blood of Christ and through his saints whose ministry of love is eternal, and he lets our spirituality grow through physical media. We celebrate God in full expressions of joy in beautiful worship through the material symbols that the church has used for centuries. The beads of the Rosary are physical, but represent the spiritual. Each bead is a tangible prayer that can be felt both physically and spiritually.

All people who are truly seeking God will find him. In having written this book, I encourage all Anglicans and Catholics, and indeed all Christians, to use it as a means of spiritual development and it is my sincere hope that in doing so, all will look upon Mary as a special friend and she will find a place in the hearts of all people.

If this little book succeeds in bringing some people closer to God, then it will have achieved its purpose.

SUGGESTIONS FOR SAYING THE ROSARY

The Rosary is prayer and must be said reverently and thoughtfully, otherwise it becomes meaningless. It is important to be comfortable when praying and meditating, so it is suggested that you sit rather than kneel. As you turn your thoughts towards God, breathe deeply and let your whole body become completely relaxed.

I have written the prayers of the Rosary in the first person singular, because it is the individual's approach to God, seeking to develop his/her personal spiritual life. When the Rosary is said by groups, or used in congregational worship in church, it is appropriate to use the plural form.

The Rosary covers the main events of our Lord's life and is divided into five decades, which are:

1. The Joyful Events
2. The Teaching Years
3. The Loving Signs
4. The Sorrowful Events
5. The Glorious Events

It is not intended that the whole Rosary be said at any one time, but rather one decade should be said on each occasion. When decades are said at different times, it is appropriate to say the introduction before the decade. Any decade can be said during any liturgical season, but the following is a suggested pattern.

DAY	Advent until Lent	Lent until Good Friday	Easter until Pentecost	Ordinary Times
Sunday	Joyful	Sorrowful	Glorious	Glorious
Monday	Teaching	Sorrowful	Teaching	Joyful
Tuesday	Joyful	Teaching	Glorious	Teaching
Wednesday	Joyful	Sorrowful	Glorious	Sorrowful
Thursday	Loving	Loving	Loving	Loving
Friday	Sorrowful	Sorrowful	Sorrowful	Sorrowful
Saturday	Glorious	Joyful	Glorious	Glorious

How often should you pray the Rosary? This, of course, is up to the individual depending on opportunity, but it is important to adopt a rule of life and establish a definite pattern of prayer.

It is appropriate to offer the Rosary for a special intention. Intentions could include special thanksgiving, intercessions, penance, etc.

After each prayer there is a reflection on that prayer and the events surrounding the topic of the prayer. To reflect, close your eyes, breathe deeply, and let a mental image build up in your mind, listen to Jesus as he talks to you in your thoughts and then talk to Christ of the things in your heart.

When the Rosary is said in a group, individuals could offer the particular prayer and share images with the others. When said in congregational worship, the leader could suggest images for reflection.

We say the Rosary to worship God and to honour Mary. We encounter Christ in the Rosary and we draw closer to him. In our prayers we grow in love and compassion which are essential in the development of the spiritual life. God is seeking our spiritual awareness and I commend the use of the Rosary as an excellent means of achieving this goal.

Peace and blessings be with you as you pray the Rosary and worship God and ask the Blessed Virgin Mary to intercede for you and feel engulfed by their all-consuming love.

INTRODUCTION

At the cross, kissing it as a mark of love and devotion to our Lord, make the sign of the cross and say: "In the name of the Father, and of the Son, and of the Holy Spirit. Amen.

"Father, I offer this meditation as an act of worship as I reflect on the life of your Beloved Son, Our Lord Jesus Christ, and ask the intercession of the Blessed Virgin Mary, His Mother. Amen."
(Here mention your special intentions).

Modern Lord's Prayer

Our Father in heaven, hallowed be your name, your kingdom come, your will be done on earth as in heaven. Give us today our daily bread. Forgive us our sins as we forgive those who sin against us. Save us from the time of trial (Lead us not into temptation,) and deliver us from evil. For the kingdom, the power, and the glory are yours now and for ever. Amen.

Traditional Lord's Prayer

Our Father, which art in heaven, Hallowed be thy name, thy kingdom come, thy will be done on earth, as it is in heaven. Give us this day our daily bread. And forgive us our trespasses, as we forgive them that trespass against us. And lead us not into temptation; But deliver us from evil. For thine is the kingdom, the power and the glory, forever and ever. Amen

Apostles Creed

I believe in God, the Father Almighty, maker of heaven and earth; and in Jesus Christ, his only Son our Lord, who was conceived by the Holy Spirit, born of the virgin Mary, suffered under Pontius Pilate, was crucified, died and was buried.

He descended to the dead. On the third day he rose from the dead. He ascended into heaven, and is seated at the right hand of God the Father Almighty; from there he shall come to judge the living and the dead. I believe in the Holy Spirit, the holy catholic church, the communion of saints, the forgiveness of sins, the resurrection of the body, and the life everlasting.

Amen

2. I praise you dear Father for all your creation and thank you that you love me and made me. Blessed be God forever.

Reflection

All glory and praise to you, my beloved Father.

3. I praise you beloved Jesus, my brother, for you showed me what Our Father is really like. You died and rose to show me that I have eternal life. All glory and praise to you, Lord Jesus Christ, my Saviour.

Reflection

Blessed be God forever.

4. I praise you beloved Holy Spirit because you live in me and are making me holy. Praised and adored be God the Holy Spirit forever.

Reflection

All glory and praise to you Lord Spirit

5. Glory be to the Father, and to the Son, and to the Holy Spirit; as it was in the beginning, is now and ever shall be, forever and ever.

Amen

At the medal say:

Beloved Mary, you brought Jesus, my brother, into this world, cared for him and brought him to manhood; I ask your prayers that I too may grow to the fullness of his stature and I say:

Hail Mary, full of grace, the Lord is with you; blessed are you among women, and blessed is the fruit of your womb Jesus. Holy Mary, Mother of God, pray for us sinners now and at the hour of our death.

Amen

THE JOYFUL EVENTS

THE FIRST DECADE

1. Dear Mary, the angel of the Lord appeared to you and you accepted the glorious honour of being the Mother of God's Son.

O Lord, you are full of steadfast love and compassion for your people.

Reflection

Hail Mary ...

2. Mary, your husband Joseph received the word of the Lord from an angel and, as an obedient servant of God, became the earthly father of the Christ.

Speak to me, Lord, your servant is listening.

Reflection

Hail Mary ...

3. Blessed Mary, when you visited your cousin Elizabeth, the unborn John the Baptist recognised his Lord even from the womb.

Blessed Lord, your Holy Spirit lives with all those who love you.

Reflection

Hail Mary ...

4. Blessed Mary, you made the long trip with Joseph from Nazareth to Bethlehem and gave birth to the Saviour of the world in a lowly stable.

Dear Lord, grant that I may always offer you myself as a place in which to dwell.

Reflection

Hail Mary ...

5. Wrapped in swaddling clothes, foreshadowing his body being wrapped in a shroud, Mary, you laid your little Son in an animal's feed-box.

O Lord, teach me to be truly humble.

Reflection

Hail Mary ...

6. Shepherds and visitors from the East came to worship your Son, Mary, and brought him precious gifts, but your gift to the world, the Christ, is a gift without equal.

Blessed Christ, please accept my life as a living sacrifice, as I live and work for your praise and glory.

Reflection

Hail Mary...

7. Mary, at the end of eight days, you and Joseph had your baby Son circumcised according to the law and named him Jesus as the angel of the Lord commanded.

Grant, O Father, that the name of your beloved Son will always be in my mind, on my lips and in my heart in loving prayer.

Reflection

Hail Mary ...

8. Dearest Mary, you and Joseph went to Jerusalem to give thanks to the Lord at the temple for the birth of your baby Son, and Simeon, the old man, took Jesus in his arms and proclaimed him to be the Christ.

Beloved Jesus, I proclaim you Lord of my life forever.

Reflection

Hail Mary ...

9. Mary, when you, Joseph and baby Jesus left Jerusalem, you returned to Nazareth and lived there as a Holy Family.

Lord Christ, I pray that my family and I will always strive to serve you and each other in true holiness.

Reflection

Hail Mary ...

10. Mary, how well you remember when Jesus was twelve and he became separated from you and Joseph in the crowd. How anxious you were for three days until you found him with the learned men in his Father's house. How dearly you held all these things in your heart.

Blessed Jesus, sometimes I too get lost, but grant that I may never lose you.

Reflection

Hail Mary ...

As I think upon the events of your early life, Lord Jesus Christ, as you grew up in Nazareth with your holy parents, I say blessed be God for all his gifts, through Christ our Lord. Amen.

and/or

Glory be to the Father, and to the Son, and to the Holy Spirit, as it was in the beginning, is now and ever shall be, forever and ever. Amen.

Kiss the crucifix, make the sign of the cross and say: Thank you my beloved Lord for this most precious time we have spent together. Blessed be God forever.

THE TEACHING YEARS

SECOND DECADE

1. Dear Mary, how sad you were when Jesus left home, but you knew that he had to do his Father's work. He was constantly in your thoughts and prayers, as he is in mine.

Glory and praise to you, Lord Jesus Christ.

Reflection

Hail Mary ...

2. O sinless Jesus, you identified so closely with your sinful people that, on their behalf, you were baptised at John's hands and received your Father's divine approval.

Blessed Christ, in my baptism I also renounced sin, and I pray that my body may always be the dwelling place of the Holy Spirit.

Glory and praise to you, Lord Jesus Christ.

Reflection

Hail Mary ...

3. Dearest Mary, how happy you were when Jesus returned home to visit you, Joseph and the family, but how sad you must have been when the townspeople rejected him and tried to kill him.

The Lord is kind and merciful.

Reflection

Hail Mary ...

4. Dear Jesus, as you set out on your ministry, you called your disciples to follow you. You first called Peter, James and John, and then others, and you are calling others today. Holy Christ, may I ever hear your call and respond to it. Lord, here am I, send me.

Blessed be God forever.

Reflection

Hail Mary ...

5. Lord Jesus, as you travelled around from town to town, you met many types of people. Some acknowledged that they were sinners and listened to your teaching, but many considered themselves already holy and your words fell on deaf ears.

Jesus, I acknowledge my sinfulness and pray that I may always be ready to hear your word and do it and become the person you want me to be.

Glory and praise to you, Lord Jesus Christ.

Reflection

Hail Mary ...

6. Lord Jesus, on the mount of transfiguration you showed the glorious radiance of your holiness to your friends. May I, beloved Lord, let your light shine in my life, that all may see that I have been with you, may see my good works and glorify our Father.

Praise to you, Lord Jesus Christ, King of endless glory.

Reflection

Hail Mary ...

7. Lord Christ, you taught your disciples that true greatness lies in service. Help me not to seek the places of honour in life, but as a child of faith, to do great things in your name.

O Sinless Servant, help me to be like you.

Reflection

Hail Mary ...

8. Dear Lord, you sent your disciples out to preach the gospel and to heal the sick. May I, your disciple in this place, be ever mindful of my ministry and in my life proclaim your good news.

Blessed be God forever.

Reflection

Hail Mary ...

9. Dear Mary, at the wedding in Cana in Galilee, you asked help of your Son for those who were in need, and he never failed them. Beloved Mother, I constantly need Jesus' help as I grow into a truly spiritual person. I ask you to intercede for me also, a person in need.

Lord, you are kind and merciful.

Reflection

Hail Mary...

10. Beloved brother, Son of God, you showed the power and love of our Father in all the miracles you performed. Let me constantly be aware that my body of flesh can be miraculously changed to be born again in the spirit and enter the kingdom of God in its fullness. Lord, let me be transformed by the renewal of my mind.

Praised and adored be God the Holy Spirit forever.

Reflection

Hail Mary ...

As I reflect on the events of your teaching years, beloved Jesus, I say blessed be God for all his gifts, through Christ our Lord. Amen.

and/or

Glory be to the Father, and to the Son, and to the Holy Spirit, as it was in the beginning, is now and ever shall be, forever and ever. Amen.

Kiss the crucifix, make the sign of the cross and say: Thank you Lord for listening to me. I know you always hear and answer my prayers. Blessed be God forever.

THE LOVING SIGNS

THE THIRD DECADE

1. Dear Lord Jesus, your whole life was full of signs of your love for us, for you are the Father's Sacrament sent to enlighten the world.

My heart is filled with love and thankfulness as I reflect on the wonderful sacraments you have given for the spiritual growth of the world.

Blessed be God forever.

Reflection

Hail Mary ...

BAPTISM

2. Dear Christ, you were baptised to identify yourself with your sinful people. I thank you for my Baptism into your Body, the Church, and that I have been born again by water and the Spirit.

All glory and praise to you, Lord Jesus Christ.

Reflection

Hail Mary ...

CONFIRMATION

3. Beloved Lord Jesus, there is great power in your hands, and we are filled and strengthened by the Holy Spirit through the hands of Confirmation. Grant that I may live my life in the power of your Holy Spirit and be constantly aware of your indwelling presence.

Blessed be God forever.

Reflection

Hail Mary ...

HOLY COMMUNION

4. O Lord, you said that whoever eats your Body and drinks your Blood has eternal life. Blessed Jesus, I know that you are the Bread of Life and that I have the fullness of life in you.

Thank you for this most precious gift, O Lamb of God.

Reflection

Hail Mary ...

CONFESSION

5. Lord, you love me and I love you, but sometimes I sin. Thank you for your great gift of loving forgiveness when I repent, confess my sins and change my life. Blessed Saviour, let me always remember that if I want forgiveness, I must also be ready to forgive those who wrong me.

Lord, let me be a forgiving person.

Reflection

Hail Mary ...

ORDINATION

6. Beloved Lord, it is your will that your Church on Earth continue to grow and flourish. We acknowledge that all of us who bear the name of Christ are a priesthood of believers and share in your ministry. I pray that your love will touch the hearts and minds of many to offer themselves in special ministry as your ordained servants.

Blessed be God forever.

Reflection

Hail Mary ...

MARRIAGE

7. Dear Mary, you were joined to Joseph in a loving relationship of holy Marriage and lived as a Holy Family. I pray that all couples who are joined together as one will express in their lives the richness of the love that you and Joseph shared and always find Christ at the centre of their marriage.

Blessed be God forever

Reflection

Hail Mary ...

HOLY UNCTION

8. O Lord, in our human bodies we suffer sickness, pain and death. I thank you for your healing grace received through the prayerful laying on of hands and Holy Unction. All people have the assurance of your healing and forgiveness, and for this, I thank you, Lord.

Blessed be God forever.

Reflection

Hail Mary ...

9. I thank you Lord, for all your saints and guardian angels who pray for us, guide us and protect us on our earthly journeys. Through their intercession and love, I have the assurance of your perpetual presence.

Blessed be God forever.

Reflection

Hail Mary ...

10. I thank you for the grace that flows through your sacraments, O Lord, for they are to me signs of your endless love, assuring me of your constant presence in my life as I too become a living sacrament in you.

Glory and praise to you, O Light of the World.

Reflection

Hail Mary ...

As I think upon all these loving signs of your endless grace, brother Jesus, I say blessed be God for all his gifts, through Christ our Lord. Amen.

and/or

Glory be to the Father, and to the Son, and to the Holy Spirit, as it was in the beginning, is now, and ever shall be, forever and ever. Amen.

Kiss the crucifix, make the sign of the cross and say: Thank you, Holy Trinity, for the honour and privilege of letting me speak with you in prayer. Blessed be God forever.

THE SORROWFUL EVENTS

THE FOURTH DECADE

1. Lord Jesus, on Palm Sunday you entered Jerusalem to the cheers of people who proclaimed you as their King but later rejected you, not understanding your mission. Grant, O Lord, that I who proclaim you King, may understand my mission of love and truly do your will in my life.

Praise to you, Lord Jesus Christ, King of endless glory.

Reflection

Hail Mary ...

2. Beloved Lord, you entered our Father's house of prayer and were rightly angry when you found that men had turned it into a marketplace. Gracious Saviour, always cleanse the temple of my body that your light of love will ever shine in me, and that all may see my good works, know that I have been with you and glorify our Father.

All glory and praise to you, blessed Jesus, the Light of the world.

Reflection

Hail Mary ...

3. Beloved Christ, Bread of Heaven, at your Last Supper you gave your disciples your Body and Blood and commanded them to love one another. Grant, O Lord, that I may always so venerate this Blessed Sacrament, that I may ever see within myself the fruit of your redemption.

All glory and praise to you, O Lamb of God.

Reflection

Hail Mary ...

4. Brother Jesus, in the garden you made your anguished prayer that our Father's will would be done for you. Lord, may I ever be a watchful servant and be ready, like you, to accept the Father's will in my life.

Blessed be God forever.

Reflection

Hail Mary ...

5. Lord of Life, you were delivered into the hands of sinful men for material gain; I pray that I will not set my heart on earthly things, but will always find my treasure in you. Lord, I know that you love me.

Blessed be God forever.

Reflection

Hail Mary ...

6. At your trial, O Lord, all deserted you. You were spat on, mocked, whipped and forced to wear a cruel crown of thorns. Blessed Saviour, the sins of the world brought all this suffering upon you; always keep me from sin.

Be merciful, O Lord, for I have sinned.

Reflection

Hail Mary ...

7. Peter, through fear you denied your beloved Lord, yet you wept bitterly after looking into his eyes. I have the same weaknesses as you had, Peter, but with God's love in my heart, may my weakness be turned into strength just as yours was.

The Lord is kind and merciful.

Reflection

Hail Mary ...

8. Beloved Lord Christ, after your cruel scourging you carried the heavy cross of my sin and stumbled and fell under its great weight. Brother Jesus, as I bear my crosses in life and stumble and fall, pick me up again, O Lord, that I may die to sin and live for you.

Merciful Saviour of the world, walk with me through this earthly life.

Reflection

Hail Mary…

9. Beloved Lord, at Golgotha you were nailed to the cross and your precious blood flowed from your pierced body. As I reflect on your great act of love, I say, O Lamb of God, you take away the sin of the world, have mercy on us; O Lamb of God, you take away the sin of the world, have mercy on us; O Lamb of God, you take away the sin of the world, grant us your peace.

Lord, you are full of love and compassion.

Reflection

Hail Mary ...

10. Dearest Mary, you stood broken-hearted at the foot of the cross watching your beloved Son's life stream from his pierced body. How the memories of his childhood and later life must have passed through your mind as you shared in his agony. How shattered you were when they laid his lifeless body in that cold tomb.

Into your hands, O Lord, I commend my spirit.

Reflection

Hail Mary ...

Blessed Father, as I reflect on your redeeming love in giving your Son for the sins of the world, I say blessed be God for all his gifts, through Christ our Lord. Amen.

and/or

Glory be to the Father, and to the Son, and to the Holy Spirit, as it was in the beginning, is now, and ever shall be, forever and ever. Amen.

Kiss the crucifix, make the sign of the cross and say: Thank you Holy Trinity for your endless love and constant presence in my life. Blessed be God forever.

THE GLORIOUS EVENTS

THE FIFTH DECADE

1. Dear Mary Magdalene, it was with great sadness in your hearts on that Sunday morning that you and the other women went to the tomb to embalm Jesus' body; but great was your surprise and joy to see your Lord alive and well.

All glory and praise to you, my risen Saviour.

Reflection

Hail Mary ...

2. Beloved Mary Magdalene, how frustrated you were when even the Lord's apostles would not believe that you had seen the risen Christ. Peter and John, how puzzled you were when you saw the empty tomb. Lord, when the frustrations of life cloud my understanding, strengthen me in the power of your risen life to remember and accept the truth of your holy word.

Blessed be God forever.

Reflection

Hail Mary ...

3. Beloved Christ, on the road to Emmaus your two disciples only recognised you in the breaking of the bread. I pray, Lord, that as I talk with you my heart will always burn within me as I am filled with joy in living as a child of the resurrection.

Blessed, praised and adored be our God forever.

Reflection

Hail Mary ...

4. Dear Lord Jesus, how scared your friends were when you appeared to them on that Sunday evening as they hid behind locked doors. You gave them your peace, you breathed your Holy Spirit on them and changed their disbelief into overwhelming joy. Lord Christ, grant that I who love you may ever be full of faith and the Holy Spirit, and always be blessed with your peace.

Glory and praise to you, beloved brother, Jesus.

Reflection

Hail Mary ...

5. Lord Christ, your apostle Thomas would not believe that you had been raised to life until he saw you and your cruel wounds. Thomas, you saw Jesus, you believed and proclaimed him your Lord and God. I have not seen your risen body, O Lord, but full of faith and happiness, I too proclaim you as my Lord and my God.

Blessed be God forever.

Reflection

Hail Mary...

6. Beloved Mary, how overcome with joy you were when you saw and embraced your mysterious Son after his resurrection. The angel of the Lord told you all those years ago that your Son would be "God with us". I too rejoice with you as I think of his eternal love and presence with me and all people.

The Lord is almighty and worthy of all praise, glory and adoration.

Reflection

Hail Mary ...

7. O Peter, how happy you and the others were to see your Master on the seashore and to eat with him; but how sad you were when Jesus, our brother, asked you if you loved him. Beloved Christ, I love you, but sometimes I act as if I don't. Grant that I may never grieve you, but always be full of love for you and all people.

Blessed be God forever.

Reflection

Hail Mary ...

8. Blessed Jesus, after your resurrection you were seen by many people to bring them to the fullness of faith. You then returned to the presence of our Father to prepare a place for us all. I praise you, O Lord, for your glorious Ascension and I know that you will never leave us comfortless because you are with us always, even to the end of time.

All glory and praise to you, Lord Jesus Christ.

Reflection

Hail Mary ...

9. Beloved Lord, at Pentecost you fulfilled your promise by sending to us the Comforter, the Spirit of Truth. May I, like the apostles, always be a Spirit-filled person ready and eager to do your will in my life.

Praised and adored be God the Holy Spirit forever.

Reflection

Hail Mary ...

10. Blessed Mary, when your earthly journey came to an end, you joined Jesus and Joseph and all your other loved ones in the eternal presence of God, our Father. We who are still on Earth need your constant intercession. Please pray for us.

Blessed, praised and honoured be the most holy Mother of our Lord, now and forever.

Reflection

Hail Mary…

(At the cross)
As I reflect on the glorious events, beloved Lord Jesus, of our Father's love for us all, I say blessed be God for all his gifts, through Christ our Lord. Amen.

and/or

Glory be to the Father, and to the Son, and to the Holy Spirit, as it was in the beginning, is now, and ever shall be, forever and ever. Amen.

Kiss the crucifix, make the sign of the cross and say: Thank you, Lord God, for the privilege of saying this Rosary and speaking with Blessed Mary and your other holy ones in prayer. Blessed be God forever.

INVITATION FROM ST LUKE'S HEALING FOUNDATION

St Luke's Healing Foundation is a not-for-profit, tax-deductible charity whose mission is to help homeless and disadvantaged young people. The number of youth requiring support is constantly growing and the Foundation is totally focused on its project, 'Youth Outreach Australia' to help these young people in Australia.

Please consider becoming a donor/benefactor to support the 'Youth Outreach Australia' project and help these young people to achieve a good quality of life and a positive future.

Reflect on the words of Jesus on 'The Final Judgement' recorded in Matthew 25:34: "The King will say to the people on his right, 'Come, you that are blessed by my Father! Come and possess the kingdom which has been prepared for you ever since the creation of the world. For I was hungry and you fed me, thirsty and you gave me a drink; I was a stranger and you received me in your homes, naked and you clothed me; I was sick and you took care of me, in prison and you visited me.' The righteous will then answer him, 'When, Lord, did we ever see you hungry and feed you, or thirsty and give you a drink? When did we ever see you a stranger and welcome you in our homes, or naked and clothe you?' The King will reply, 'I tell you, whenever you did this to one of the least important of these my brethren, you did it to me!'"

DONATIONS to the Foundation can be made by phoning FREECALL 1800 007915 or on our website www.stlukeshf.org through the secure Paypal system. You can also make a donation at any branch of the Commonwealth Bank of Australia or by mail to: 10 Jordan Close, North Rockhampton, Queensland. Australia, 4701.

Please also remember the work of the Foundation in your Will. For further details, please email us on stlukeshf@internode.net.au

www.ingramcontent.com/pod-product-compliance
Ingram Content Group UK Ltd.
Pitfield, Milton Keynes, MK11 3LW, UK
UKHW040028200726
13854UKWH00001B/416

9 780852 441565